Path of the Spirit

Path of the Spirit

Dr. Judy Baus

Path of The Spirit

New King James Version of The Holy Bible used where Scripture is referenced.

Published with CreateSpace on Amazon.com. Stock image of Dove of Peace courtesy of all-free-download.com.

Edited by Lynda Johnson.

Cover design by Tracy Foster-Pyke.

Book Coordination by Kimberly Thompson. All rights reserved.

ISBN-13: 978-1542812719

ISBN-10: 1542812712

1. Religion; Christian Ministry
2. Discipleship

Contents

Contents

Introduction

Path of the Spirit is one of the most powerful and practical books I've edited. In the early days of Good News Ministries, I remember Judy's concern over where funds would come from to repair their first ministry bus. The bus wasn't in as pristine condition as promised over the phone, which Vic soon learned when he flew to Oklahoma to drive it home. It kept breaking down along the way, with repairs into several thousand dollars. Where would that money come from? Judy and Vic had given up their jobs and moved to San Jose to attend Bible college. Things were tight. Judy and those around her prayed for the funds to pay for the repairs. As she watched God supply for this huge (to her) amount, Judy's faith grew to trust for bigger things.

Those were the initial stages of Judy's learning to listen to and trust the Holy Spirit. And now, 24 years later, she and Vic have had many opportunities to grow in their walk with the Spirit. They are still in ministry, still traveling two buses later, and still teaching others about God's faithfulness and how to listen to and trust the Holy Spirit's leading. This book shows the vital role the Spirit has in a Christian's life and how it is impossible to live victoriously without Him, yet how natural it can become to walk in the Spirit day after day as we seek this kind of life.

Judy Baus is director and co-founder of Good News Ministries, Inc., a *giving* ministry that she and her husband Vic began more than 24 years ago. The ministry serves the mission field of America. In their reconstructed MCI bus, Judy and Vic travel the country introducing Jesus to those who don't know Him, reintroducing Jesus to those who once knew Him, and sharing more of Jesus with those who do know Him. They also reach out to help those in need with clothing and food.

Judy's sensitivity and obedience to the Holy Spirit brings restoration, healing, and deliverance. As she flows in the gifts of the Spirit, she ministers with simplicity, clarity, and accuracy to bring about change in peoples' lives!

Lynda Johnson,
Editor

"Now may the God of hope fill you with all joy and peace in believing, that you may abound in hope by the power of the Holy Spirit." Romans 15:13

Path of the Spirit is Judy's fourth published book. Her first book, *From Rags to Riches,* chronicles her own personal story of salvation and deliverance. The second book is titled *Faith, Does it Really Move Mountains?* and her third book, *On the Road Again with God*, which highlights 31 lessons learned on the road.

Notes

Foreword

The path of the Spirit is a mystery to some people, and an intrigue to others. Is God's Spirit alive and active in our world today? If so, in what way? Does the Spirit affect the events of our world or even our very personal lives? I shall attempt to answer these questions by going to Scripture itself. You will soon see that this book is *not* a light reading; rather, it is an in-depth study of the Person of the Holy Spirit. A believer who wants a deeper walk with God needs to know about the Holy Spirit and His God-ordained role in the Christian's life and in the world today.

Jesus let us know that His followers would be hated (not just disliked!) by the world (John 15:18-20). Hatred and persecution of believers have been going on for centuries in other countries, but it is happening more and more in our own country as America is turning away from God and the values found in the Bible. Christians in America are being mocked for our faith, ridiculed for our "narrow-mindedness," and discriminated against by society. But Jesus reminds us, *"You are of God, little children, and have overcome them, because He who is in you is greater than he who is in the world."* (1 John 4:4).

Jesus told us that His followers are IN the world but not OF the world, so how are we to live above the persecution and hatred? John answered this by saying that it is something on the *inside* of the believer that is greater than whatever is happening around him. What is this greatness on the inside of the child of God? It is a person, the person of the Holy Spirit.

As we study the work of the Spirit, we will see how He helps us live in this world true to God and to our desire to love and obey Him, no matter what. My passion is to see every child of God understand and follow the path of the Holy Spirit. That is why I have written this book…to help all who want to live a victorious life in Christ, not *somehow,* but *triumphantly.*

In Christ,
Dr. Judy Baus

Notes

Notes

Chapter 1

Background on the Holy Spirit

"In the beginning...."
(Genesis 1)

The Bible reveals the activity of the Holy Spirit from Genesis to Revelation, both in creation and redemption. He was involved in creation: *"In the beginning God created the heavens and the earth. The earth was without form, and void; and darkness was on the face of the deep. And the Spirit of God was hovering over the face of the waters."* (Genesis 1:1-2). The last mention of the Holy Spirit is found in Revelation 22:17: *"And the Spirit and the bride say, Come! And let him who hears say, Come! And let him who thirsts come. Whoever desires, let him take the water of life freely."*

The Holy Spirit is mentioned more than 90 times in the Old Testament with at least 18 titles given to Him. In the New Testament the Holy Spirit is mentioned more than 260 times with 39 names and titles. Out of the 27 books of the New Testament, II John and III John are the only books with no reference to the Holy Spirit. Joel 2:28 says, *"And it shall come to pass afterward that I will pour out My Spirit on all flesh..."* This foretold the coming of *the last days* when the Spirit would be poured out upon all flesh, in contrast to Old Testament times when the Spirit was only available for specific purposes to a select few in Israel. The Church must not lose sight of the Holy Spirit's vital role in this dispensation of grace or it will become devoid of spiritual power.

The vast resources of the Spirit are for each person in the Body of Christ, not just for a few believers. If we do not have the proper knowledge and understanding concerning the teaching of the Holy Spirit, we will become ineffective and a victim instead of a victor in this life. As we learn to appreciate, experience, know, and understand the person, work, and ministry of the Spirit, we will learn to function effectively as a child of God in the world today. Redemption is the process needed to become a child of God, but the ministry of the Holy Spirit in a believer's life will keep him on his path of destiny and purpose. It is the Spirit who reveals the Father and the Son (John 14:15-26). The fullness of the Spirit, with His gifts and fruit, is to be received and embraced by every member of the Body of Christ always.

Any study of the Spirit is more or less imperfect because of man's inability to describe and understand an infinite God. However, every statement can be backed up by Scripture. The Father, the Son, and the Spirit are one and only one God. Neither is God without the others, and each with the others is God. The Father says "I," the Son says "I," and the Spirit says "I." The Father loves the Son—the Son honors the Father—the Spirit testifies of the Son.

In the following pages we will see how the Holy Spirit helps the believer bring the works of Jesus to a world that so desperately needs Him. It is only by the Spirit that the believer can live triumphantly through Christ in this world.

Notes

Chapter 2

Introducing the Holy Spirit

"It seemed good to the Holy Spirit, and to us...."
(Acts 15:28)

Throughout Scripture the Holy Spirit is given high importance. Sadly, we can't say that the Church has given Him the same importance because throughout history, the Spirit has been downplayed in most denominations. One of the great Puritan writers, Thomas Goodwin, said that most Christians in his day (A.D. 1660) did not give the Holy Spirit the glory due Him. "Some hardly even mentioned Him. It was almost as if the Spirit was forgotten."

In the nineteenth century many people openly denied that the Holy Spirit was a real person or that He was God. Even in the early part of the 20th century when the Pentecostal revival was spreading, some were saying that the gifts and ministry of the Holy Spirit were of no interest to the Church. Contrary to this, Evangelist Dwight L. Moody said, "If we are full of pride and conceit and ambition and self-seeking and pleasure of the world, there is no room for the Spirit of God, and I believe many a man is praying to God to fill him when he is full already with something else." Thankfully today we see an increased interest in the Holy Spirit.

The doctrine of the Holy Spirit is called *pneumatology*. The Bible teaches that the Holy Trinity (the Father, the Son, and the Spirit) is one and only one God. The Holy Spirit is equal with the Father and Son in all their divine attributes.

Even though the Father, Son, and Holy Spirit are equal in all their divine attributes, they each have characteristics that the other does not have, and still is only one God. This is somewhat mysterious because we are trying to comprehend an infinite God with a finite mind. The Holy Spirit is the third person of the Godhead who is still at work in the hearts and lives of men and women all over the world. It is important to understand His nature and His work in order to understand how He will work in our lives as we yield ourselves to Him (1 Corinthians 2:12).

First-century believers had a wonderful relationship with the Holy Spirit. They based their decisions on what the Holy Spirit wanted. This can be observed during the first Council of the Early Church, called the Jerusalem Council. At that time, the first Gentiles were believing and coming into the

Church. The question put before the Council was whether or not the new Gentile believers had to follow the Law of Moses to be saved. Paul and Barnabas had seen the miracles God was performing among the Gentiles and they told of them. After some discussion among the Jewish believers and leaders of the Church, they came to an agreement: *"For it seemed good to the Holy Spirit, and to us…"* (see Acts 15:7, 8, 28). This shows clearly that first-century believers submitted to the direction and guidance of the Holy Spirit. He was a reality in their lives, just as the Spirit must be a reality in the lives of believers today. For this to happen, we must study and understand who He is, what He does, and why and how He does it.

Notes

Chapter 3

The Illuminator of God's Will

"But the Helper, the Holy Spirit, whom the Father will send in My name, He will teach you all things, and bring to your remembrance all things that I said to you."
(John 14:26)

The Holy Spirit used men to write the Bible, but He is the author. When we read the Bible, remember that we are reading what the Spirit wrote so we need His illumination to understand it.

It is also the Holy Spirit's job to illuminate Jesus to us. Jesus says in John 14:23, *"...If anyone loves Me, he will keep My word; and My Father will love him, and We will come to him and make Our home with him."* This Scripture clearly shows the oneness of the Trinity, referring to the whole Godhead; Father, Son, and Holy Spirit.

While Jesus Christ was on earth He was guiding His disciples, but He also taught them concerning the Spirit who would continue to guide them after His departure. He knew He was going back to the Father and that the disciples would carry on the birthing and growth of the Church. Jesus tells His followers in John 14:12, *"Most assuredly, I say to you, he who believes in Me, the works that I do he will do also; and greater works than these he will do, because I go to My Father."*

I can almost hear the disciples protest – GREATER works? How can that be? Because of the number of believers working together doing the works of Jesus, the *quantity* will be greater, but not the *quality*.

Jesus adds, *"These things I have spoken to you while being present with you. But the Helper, the Holy Spirit, whom the Father will send in My name, He will teach you all things and bring to your remembrance all things that I said to you."* (John 14: 25, 26). If Jesus told the disciples that the Holy Spirit would comfort, help, bring truth, and teach them, then how much more does the believer who lives in the world today need the Holy Spirit? Believers have been given the duty to carry on the works of Jesus and in order to accomplish that work, we need the Holy Spirit to direct us. The Holy Spirit is preparing a triumphant Church of the Lord Jesus Christ to celebrate the coronation of the King of kings. The Holy Spirit proceeds from the Father and is sent by Jesus Christ (John 14:26; John 15:26). The Church is to go forth and present Jesus Christ to the world and not stumble when doing it. Who is the Church? It is those who believe that Jesus Christ is the Messiah and follow Him. Jesus tells His believers that the Holy Spirit will keep them from stumbling at doing the work of His ministry (John 16:1).

Jesus talks about believers being co-laborers with Him but they are also co-laborers with the Holy Spirit. Over and over Jesus tells His people that the Holy Spirit is the Spirit of Truth, and the Holy Spirit will glorify Jesus. The Holy Spirit will declare all things to the Church corporately and individually. There is nothing going on in the spirit realm that will not be declared to the believer because it is the job of the Holy Spirit to declare it to him. The word *all* in John 16:15 (in the Greek and any other language) means just that, *all*. The Holy Spirit will declare to the child of God the good things and the bad things, but we have to be hearing what the Spirit is saying to us.

There is a real devil, real demons, and they have real plans against us. The corporate Church and the individual believer have a responsibility to use the Word of God to dismantle the plans of the enemy as declared to them by the Holy Spirit. In the same way, true Christians have a responsibility to walk in the plan of God as the Holy Spirit reveals it to us.

A key function of the Holy Spirit is found in the words of Jesus, *"A little while, and you will not see Me; and again a little while, and you will see Me, because I go to the Father."* (John 16:16). Jesus is saying that His ascension from the earth would take Him back to the Father from where He came, and the disciples would see Him in the flesh no more. But through the Holy Spirit, Jesus would be with them and with all believers down through time. This is music to my ears because we live in a very evil world.

Notes

Notes

Chapter 4

The Personality of the Holy Spirit

"Now the Spirit expressly says that in latter times some will depart from the faith, giving heed to deceiving spirits and doctrines of demons..."
(1Timothy 4:1)

The Holy Spirit, the third person of the Divine Trinity, is of tremendous importance in these uncertain times. A better understanding of His personality will open a path to a greater understanding of His working in our world and in our own life.

1. **The Holy Spirit** is not just a blessing to receive.

2. **The Holy Spirit** is not just an experience you have had.

3. **The Holy Spirit** is not a neutral gender or an impersonal pronoun—it! Rather, He is a proper noun—He! Jesus uses personal pronouns when He talks about the Holy Spirit (John 16:5-15).

4. **He is** a comforter who feels.

5. **He is** a teacher to listen to.

6. **He is** a guide to follow.

7. **The Holy Spirit is a real person**, though He is invisible. He is not seen in the physical realm but in the invisible spirit realm.

The Holy Spirit is not to be looked upon merely as an influence or impersonal force. We will be robbed from understanding who the Holy Spirit is if we think of Him only in that way. It is true that He does influence our life, but He is much more than an influence; He is the revealed power of God!

One reason we should not consider the Holy Spirit as a mere influence is because Scripture does not teach that. The Bible clearly shows the Holy Spirit to be a divine person. To think of Him as less than that will hinder our worship because true worship is a personal activity and needs a personal relationship.

God lives within the believer through the person of the Holy Spirit. It would be impossible to have a personal relationship with an impersonal force. We must know that the Holy Spirit is our friend, helper, and comforter. We have more than just an influence living within us; we have the full person of the Holy Spirit. God wants us to know and reverence the person of the Holy Spirit.

Dr. R.A. Torrey aptly wrote:

> *"If the Holy Spirit is a Divine Person and we know it not, we are robbing a Divine Being of the love and adoration which are His due. It is of the highest practical importance whether the Holy Spirit is a power that we, in our ignorance and weakness, are somehow to get hold of and use, or whether the Holy Spirit is a personal Being ... who is to get hold of us and use us. It is of the highest experimental importance .... Many can testify to the blessing that came into their lives when they came to know the Holy Spirit, not merely as a gracious influence... but as an ever-present, loving friend, and helper."*

The Holy Spirit is the creator, convictor, sealer, enabler, revealer of truth, and builder. He is called the Advocate, the same title used of Jesus. It means one who stands alongside (John 14:16). Jesus speaks of the Spirit as another comforter.

If He was but an influence, the Holy Spirit could not take the place of Jesus' personality. If He was an impersonal influence, He could not help us at all. He came to be personally associated with the same disciples that Jesus was personally associated with while He was on earth. **The Spirit came to be personally *in them* what Jesus was personally *to them*. Jesus was personally with them and the Holy Spirit has come to be personally in them and in every believer today.**

Notes

Notes

Chapter 5

Evidence of the Personality of the Holy Spirit

*"The grace of the Lord Jesus Christ, and the love of God,
and the communion of the Holy Spirit be with you all.
Amen."*
(2 Corinthians 13:14)

The Spirit of God is a Person, as much as the Father and Son are Persons, and therefore has all the sinless elements of a divine personality. Man was made in the image of God so it is sensible to draw a parallel between the personality of God and the personality of man. Personality consists of possessing mind (intellect), emotions, and will. The Holy Spirit has all three.

The Holy Spirit has a mind (Romans 8:27).
　　The Holy Spirit is the one, not man, who knows and understands the thoughts of God. The Word *mind* (*phronema*) means *way of thinking, mind-(set), aim,*

aspiration, striving. This makes it clear that the Holy Spirit has intellect.

The Holy Spirit has a will (1 Corinthians 12:11).

This refers to the spiritual gifts given to the believer by the Holy Spirit. The phrase *He wills* refers to decisions of the will after previous deliberation. This shows the power of sovereign choice and decision. The Spirit forbade Paul and his missionary team from preaching in Asia and instead sent them to Europe (Acts 16:6). Many times my husband and I have wanted to go to a specific location with the Gospel and the Holy Spirit made it clear we were not to go at that time.

The Holy Spirit has emotions (Isaiah 63:10; Ephesians 4:30-32).

He can be grieved. The word *grieve* means *to distress, vex, be sad, be in heaviness, and sorrowful.* Given the understanding of what the word grieve fully means, it is humbling to even think that a child of God has the ability to grieve the third Person of the Godhead—the Holy Spirit.

Jesus uses personal pronouns when He talks about the Holy Spirit (John 16:5-15). Just an influence or a power does not have a mind, will, and emotion. The Spirit is not merely a *something,* but a divine *Someone.* If He were only a mere influence or power, the scriptural method of describing Him would be contradictory and make no sense. When the truth of the Spirit's personality and work are understood, a life of blessedness and power opens up for the believer.

Notes

Chapter 6

A Closer Look at the Personality of the Holy Spirit

"However, when He, the Spirit of truth, has come, He will guide you into all truth..."
(John 16:13)

Personality is understood in many different ways. A blind person must feel a face or hear a voice to know someone. People are known for the way they walk and the way they talk. A mom will know her baby by the sound of the baby's cry. A person's personality is part of his movement or how he projects himself. A person can get to know the Holy Spirit also by how He moves or projects Himself which is similar to the Father and the Son.

The Holy Spirit is the head and leader of this generation.
He is the leader and out in front guiding the believer. A dog might think it is leading its owner, but the

owner is the one with the leash! A horse has a bit in its mouth with the reigns connected to the bit so the one holding the reigns is really in control and has the lead. It is the Holy Spirit who is leading and guiding the believer, and the believer is to trust the Holy Spirit to guide him to the Father and to Jesus (Romans 8:14).

He is a faithful guide.

The Holy Spirit is the believer's guide who knows the way and would never lead the believer wrong. When a person travels to an unknown territory, he would have a travel guide who knows the territory to show the way (John 16:13). I have been traveling for over 24 years preaching the Gospel and the Holy Spirit has never once led me astray!

He is a teacher.

Jesus told His disciples that when He departed, He would send them another Helper (John 14:16). The word *another* in this verse stresses that the Holy Spirit will be a Helper of the same kind as Christ. The Holy Spirit is to carry on the same teaching ministry that Christ had with His disciples (John 14:26). The Holy Spirit is both intelligent and wise. He will cause remembrance of what Jesus has said and confirm it.

As a teacher, the Holy Spirit...
- Is promised (Proverbs 1:23).

- Is the Spirit of wisdom (Isaiah 11:2; 40:13, 14).

- Reveals the things of God (1 Corinthians 2:10, 13).

- Reveals the things of Christ (John 16:14).

- Reveals the future (Luke 2:26; Acts 21:11).

- Directs the way of godliness (Isaiah 30:21; Ezekiel 36:27).

- Enables ministers to teach (1 Corinthians 12:8).

- Teaches saints how to answer persecutors (Mark 13:11; Luke 12:12).

- Directs the decisions of the Church (Acts 15:28).

- Attends to the instruction of the Churches (Revelation 2:7, 11, 29).

- Will not reveal things of the Spirit to the natural man (1 Corinthians 2:14).

The Holy Spirit is the comforter and helper.

He is caring and full of compassion (John 14:26). The word *Helper* in the Greek is *paraklētos* meaning not only to *help* but to *comfort* and *console*. To bring comfort the Holy Spirit imparts hope, joy, and peace to the believer (Romans 15:13). I cannot count the times the Holy Spirit has brought me help and comfort when others could not.

The Holy Spirit is an intercessor.

In the believer's weakness and groaning, the Holy Spirit intercedes on his behalf (Romans 8:26). When the Spirit intercedes on behalf of the believer, the Father understands and answers the prayer by making all things work together for good in our life. Even though we might not see it, God will make it work for us eventually.

He is a counselor.

The Holy Spirit counsels, communes, and fellowships with the believer. The Apostle Paul wrote, *"The grace of the Lord Jesus Christ, and the love of God, and the communion of the Holy Spirit be with you all. Amen."* (2 Corinthians 13:14). Paul wanted to make it clear to the saints that they receive from God His love, they receive from Jesus Christ grace, and from the Holy Spirit communion and fellowship. This is sometimes not understood by the believer. The Holy Spirit is a counselor who wants to counsel not only the individual but the corporate Body of Christ.

The Holy Spirit is strength and power.

He gives the believer power and makes him bold to be a witness for Jesus Christ (Acts 1:8). In this verse the word *power* in the Greek is *dunamis* meaning *miraculous ability*. The word dynamite comes from this word. Jesus was resurrected by the *dunamis* of the Holy Spirit (Romans 8:11). Praise God that the power and strength of the Holy Spirit lives in every believer to enable us to be more than overcomers in this life (1 John 4:4).

He is generous.

The Holy Spirit gives wonderful spiritual gifts, and the believer is to be fully aware that these gifts are for him (1 Corinthians 12:1). The Holy Spirit wants the believer to understand and use the gifts given to him (1 Corinthians 12:7-11). We live in a very selfish world with very selfish people, but not so with the Holy Spirit!

He gives commands.

In Acts 8:29, the Holy Spirit directed Philip to speak to the Ethiopian eunuch. The Spirit commanded that Paul and Barnabas be set apart for missionary work in Acts 13:2. After this happened, they were then sent out by the Holy Spirit to do that work (Acts 13:4). In Acts 16:6, the Holy Spirit forbade Paul and Silas from preaching in Asia.

The Holy Spirit is humble.

Divinity and humility are united in the Holy Spirit. That is a hard concept for the human mind to receive (Isaiah 57:15).

The Holy Spirit gives testimony.

The word testify is to bear witness of something and that is what Jesus said that His disciples would do concerning Himself (John 15:26, 27). The Holy Spirit gives testimony of Christ and the disciples give testimony of Christ.

He is a judge that convicts.

The Holy Spirit is both equality and justice, and will convict the world of sin (John 16:8). The word *convict* means to *point something out to someone*. As well, the Holy Spirit acts as a divine prosecutor in convicting the world concerning sin, righteousness, and judgment.

He is a builder.

The Holy Spirit builds up the individual believer and the corporate body of believers (Ephesians 2:19-22). The Spirit possesses a distinct personality with His own attributes, but does not have an earthly body as humans have. It is difficult to define personality when used of the divine Being. God the Father, God the Son, and God the Holy Spirit cannot be measured by human standards. God was not made in the image of man, but man in the image of God.

Notes

Chapter 7

Names Given to the Holy Spirit Reveal His Deity

"My people are destroyed for lack of knowledge."
(Hosea 4:6)

When a name or title is given to a person, it describes something about him. My parents named me *Judy* for the purpose of identification. I grew up and married, receiving the title of *wife*. Later I had a son and was called *mother*. Now I am the same woman holding many titles besides my name. I can also be called a *gardener* because I am responsible for taking care of a garden. I am called a *teacher* because I teach the biblical principles of God. I am called an *author* because I have published books. If I was good at sports, I would be called an athlete.

It is the same with the Person of the Holy Spirit. He has names or titles that identify Him, but He is still the same person— the Holy Spirit. We can learn much about the Holy

Spirit by studying His names and titles. Here are some of them:

Divine Agent of the Godhead.

An agent is one who acts or does business for someone else. This is what the Holy Spirit does as the third person of the Trinity (Hebrews 9:14).

God.

The Holy Spirit wanted to send Peter to speak to the Gentiles about Christ, so He spoke to him in a vision which included referring to Himself as God (Acts 11:7-12).

Spirit of God.

He dwells in the believer (1 Corinthians 3:16).

Spirit of Christ.

He is the Spirit of Christ, but also the Spirit from Christ (Romans 8:9).

Eternal Spirit.

Eternal means without beginning or ending. The Eternal Spirit is uncreated, and thus divine. He is co-eternal with the Father and the Son. It was through the Eternal Spirit that Christ offered Himself without blemish (Hebrews 9:14). The Holy Spirit had a part in the conception of Jesus (Luke 1:35). He also had a part in the death and resurrection of Jesus Christ.

Things on earth are temporary and a child of God should not give them prominence because they are passing away. The things that are eternal and of the spirit realm are the things to keep in focus. The Eternal Spirit dictated the eternal Bible (2 Peter 1:21). The Eternal Spirit is the Eternal Word (Ephesians 6:17).

Omnipotent – All-Powerful.

The prefix *omni* means *all*. The Holy Spirit is eternally existent with unlimited power (Romans 8:11; Romans 15:19). Christ cast out demons by the Spirit of God (Matthew 12:28).

Omniscient – All-Knowing.

Everything pertaining to God, Christ, satan, man, heaven, and earth, is known to the Spirit. The Holy Spirit has unlimited knowledge (1 Corinthians 2:10; Romans 8:27). Only an all-knowing God can teach people all things and then cause them to remember it when they need to. The Holy Spirit knows exactly what to pray for each believer exactly when he needs it. Jesus taught His disciples these truths in John 14:25, 26.

Omnipresent – Everywhere-Present.

Human beings can only be in one place at one time. The Holy Spirit has the ability to be everywhere at the same time, and He dwells in all believers everywhere (Psalms 139:7-12). When Jesus says He will never leave the child of God nor forsake him, it is the ever-present Holy Spirit that accomplishes this task.

Sovereign.

The Holy Spirit is called Sovereign God; which means like the Father and the Son, the Holy Spirit is superior to all other power, influence, or importance (1 Corinthians 12:11). The Apostles recognized the sovereignty of the Holy Spirit and that He has complete power to dictate (Acts 13:2, 4; 2 Corinthians 3:17; Revelation 2:7).

Spirit of Truth.

Truth is opposed to falsehood. Truth is the original intent of something. It is an agreement with fact or reality. Truth is also the quality of keeping close to fact and avoiding distortion or misrepresentation. Any form of distortion, deception, dishonesty, or deceit grieves the Holy Spirit for He is the Spirit of Truth (John 16:13).

Spirit of Glory.

The word *glory* in the Greek is *doxa* meaning *dignity, honor, praise, worship*. Earthly greed, materialism, and corrupt doctrine about prosperity are the direct opposite of what the Spirit of glory represents (1 Peter 4:14).

Spirit of Grace.

We must be careful not to insult the Spirit of Grace (Hebrews 10:29).The word for *grace* in the Greek is *charis* meaning *graciousness* of manner, especially the divine influence upon the heart and its reflection in the life of the believer.

Spirit of Wisdom and Revelation.

The Holy Spirit is grieved when a believer does not carefully read the Bible. Jesus warns in Matthew 22:29, *"You are mistaken, not knowing the Scriptures nor the power of God."* Knowledge for the believer is information learned from the Scriptures by allowing the Holy Spirit to bring revelation from the Scriptures to him. Wisdom is allowing the Holy Spirit to show us how to properly apply what we have learned in our life (Ephesians 1:17).

Spirit of Life.

He is the source of life. *"For the law of the Spirit of life in Christ Jesus has made me free from the law of sin and death."* (Romans 8:2). The word *law* in the Greek is *nomos* meaning a set of principles. The words *made free* in the Greek is *eleutheroo* meaning to liberate. The Holy Spirit liberates the believer from the dominion of sin and death. Every part of a Christian's life is to be full of new life, never allowing deadness nor lukewarmness to stay.

Spirit of Promise.

Jesus told His disciples that the Promise was from the Father and that Promise was the Holy Spirit with whom Jesus would baptize them soon. The Spirit of Promise is for every follower of Jesus (Acts 1:4, 5).

Spirit of Adoption.

"For you did not receive the spirit of bondage again to fear, but you received the Spirit of adoption by whom we cry out, 'Abba, Father'." (Romans 8:15). *Abba* is a term of Chaldean origin expressing warm affection. When a child is adopted, he receives the name, place, and privileges of a son, the same as a son by birth. When a person is born again by the Spirit of Adoption, he becomes a child of God, and all the rights and privileges of the Kingdom of God belong to him. He also now has the privilege of calling the Father *Abba*. Many people struggle in life because their natural father was not around when they were growing up. But when they become a child of God, they have a heavenly Father who cares for them and will never leave them.

Spirit of Holiness.

God is holy and totally set apart from sin and sinners. Holy is the most common adjective used for the Spirit (Romans 1:4). The word *holiness* in the Greek means *sacred – physically pure and morally blameless*. The Holy Spirit is the Spirit of holiness. Any impurity, defilement, or uncleanness distresses Him. When we understand the holiness of God, we will understand how horrible sin is. We must cry out to the Spirit of holiness to show us the holiness of God as the Prophet Isaiah did. When this takes place in us, we will say as Isaiah said, *"Woe is me, for I am undone!"* (Isaiah 6:5). The Spirit of holiness desires that each child of God come to this place concerning sin.

Comforter/Helper.

Jesus Himself gave the title of Comforter/Helper to the Holy Spirit (John 14:26). The word *comforter* in the Greek is *parakletos* meaning *one called alongside to help;* thus, a counselor. The Holy Spirit indwells the Christian to help us with our ignorance and infirmity (Romans 8:26, 27). He is the best counselor we will ever have!

Notes

Chapter 8

His Divinity is Shown in His Works

*"The Spirit of God has made me, and the breath of the
Almighty gives me life."*
(Job 33:4)

As the Agent of the Godhead, the Spirit is God in action, and He has been very active throughout history. Every child of God must know fully who the Holy Spirit is, what He has done in the past, what He is doing in the present, and what He will do in the future.

The Holy Spirit was active at the start of creation (Genesis 1:1, 2).

> Here is a picture of the Holy Spirit as a mother bird. He brooded over a chaotic condition and produced this beautiful world we live in. The Holy Spirit gave life to creation. His energy created not only the beauty of the earth, but wonders of oceans came into

existence, and the glory of the heavens (Job 26:13). The masterpiece of creation was man (Job 33:4).

The Holy Spirit was active in Jesus' birth (Matthew 1:20; Luke 1:35).

The conception of Jesus is the direct action of the Holy Spirit. Christ in His deity is eternal, but the Holy Spirit begot the sinless human nature of Christ.

The Holy Spirit is active in regeneration.

As the Spirit of Life, and able to give life, the Holy Spirit generated material and physical life at creation. He brought into being man, a life so unique and marvelous, and now He produces spiritual life in all who believe (2 Corinthians 3:6; Titus 3:5). The personal agent in the new birth is the Holy Spirit, and the Word of God is the instrument He uses (I Peter 1:23). Jesus taught that the Holy Spirit produces the new birth in that He regenerates the person (John 3:6).

The word regeneration in the Greek means a *spiritual rebirth* or *to give life*. The Holy Spirit is the agent of the new birth and causes it to take place. It is not by self-determination, it is not by any ceremonial act, and it is not by any material process that individuals enter the Kingdom of God. It is by the life-giving power of the Holy Spirit (John 1:13). The new birth or born-again experience happens by the power of the

Holy Spirit and is the counterpart of human reproduction in the physical realm. Just as human regeneration produces human life, so also spiritual regeneration produces spiritual life. Christians have both an earthly birth certificate and a spiritual birth certificate!

The Holy Spirit is the inspiration of Scripture.

When the Bible uses the word *inspire*, it means *one who is instructed by divine influence.* The writers of both the Old and New Testament were moved upon by the Spirit which meant they submitted their minds to the Spirit allowing Him to give them revelation and inspiration for the writing of the sacred Scriptures (2 Peter 1:21; 2 Timothy 3:16, 17). The word *inspiration* is made up of two words, *in* or *unto*, and *spirare,* meaning *to breathe.* So a person inspired by the Spirit is one into whom the Spirit has breathed the truth He wants him to know and declare. Truly the Bible is our only manual for success!

The Holy Spirit sanctifies.

The process of sanctification first starts when we believe and are joined to Christ and thus come to be in Christ (2 Thessalonians 2:13; 1 Peter 1:2). It is the work of the Spirit that attests, seals, and confirms grace in a believer by producing the fruit of righteousness. The Holy Spirit is absolutely holy Himself and produces this quality in the believer.

There is a progression to sanctification. When we are born again, we are instantly justified (just as if we never sinned). Our sanctification is both instant and progressive, growing into completion (2 Peter 3:18). Our character is transformed daily by the progressive work of the Holy Spirit's sanctification (2 Corinthians 3:18). Because of the progressive sanctification process of the Holy Spirit, Christians are to:

- **Increase and abound in love toward one another**. The word *increase* in the Greek means more in *quantity*, *number*, or *quality*. The word *abound* in the Greek means to be *in excess in quantity or quality* (1 Thessalonians 3:12).

- **Increase and abound more and more in the graces of the Christian life** (1 Thessalonians 4:1, 10).

The Christian life is always subject to defilement because we live in a sinful world. The life of a believer is one of an ever-increasing sense of duty, and an ever-deepening consciousness of sin. Continual growth and development in the graces and virtues in the believer's life is a must, and comes from the continued working of the Spirit in us. Holiness is being perfected in the believer (2 Corinthians 7:1). Holiness is not a mushroom growth; it grows as the coral reef grows, little by little.

Notes

Notes

Chapter 9

The Holy Spirit's Nature Seen in Symbols

"....He breathed on them, and said to them, Receive the Holy Spirit."
(John 20:22)

Just as names and titles bring us greater understanding of the Holy Spirit as a person, different symbols or emblems help us understand His nature, character, and functions. Webster's Dictionary defines the word *symbol* as a thing representing something else because of relationship, association, or convention. The Bible is the mind and will of God communicating to us, and He uses human everyday language that we can easily understand. In Scripture God uses many different symbols and metaphors to reveal Himself to the heart of man. Studying the different symbols brings to light the nature and mission of the Holy Spirit.

We see the following symbols in our everyday life to remind us throughout our day of the Holy Spirit.

- *The Dove*—represents purity, gentleness, peace, beauty, and modesty. This is the Spirit's nature and office (John 1:32).

- *A Seal*—represents authority, security, identification, genuineness, finished transaction, value, and ownership. This confirms to us God's ownership of us, His authority over us, and our security in Him (Ephesians 1:13, 4:30; 2 Corinthians 1:22).

- *Oil*—Oil represents anointing for service, healing, and light. The word *anoint* in the Greek is *chrio* meaning the idea of *contact*; to *smear* or *rub* with oil, to *consecrate* to an office or religious service.

  1. Anointing for service (Luke 4:18). The office of the prophet, of the priest, and of the king received a special anointing. This is seen in the Old Testament, but it also represents how the Holy Spirit wants to anoint the believer for service.

  2. Healing. Jesus was anointed by the Holy Spirit to heal all who were oppressed by the devil. Gladness comes with healing (Acts 10:38; Hebrews 1:9).

3. Light. Anointing brings light for understanding in all truth (1 John 2:20).

- *Water*—This is the most common symbol in the Bible representing the different ministries of the Holy Spirit. John 4:14 shows the clear, clean refreshing work of the Spirit in the heart of man. We can find water represented in many ways:

  1. **Rivers** (John 7:38-39). The earth has many rivers and not one of them is the same. Jesus spoke *rivers* being plural representing the diversity of the Spirit's activities.

  2. **Floods** (Isaiah 44:3). A flood is water coming over the ground with overwhelming volume and force. God flooded the earth with His judgment in Noah's day, and he can also flood the earth with His blessings. Floods stand for the fullness and superabundance of the Spirit's supply.

  3. **Rain** (Psalms 72:6). When the earth experiences a lack of rain, it becomes parched and famine results. When rain comes to the earth it produces life. This is the same with the Spirit who is the life-giving power of God.

  4. **Springs** (Psalms 87:7). Have you ever driven in the mountains and come upon a stream of water

flowing down the bank and forming a small pool? That is the most refreshing water I've ever tasted. It springs forth from underground. All spirituality springs forth from (is created by) the Spirit in a continual supply.

5. **Dew** (Hosea 14:5). Dew comes in the morning and can go unnoticed, yet it is still present. It is the same with the powerful effects of the Spirit.

- *Clothing*— In Luke 24:49, the word *endued* is used, and in the Greek it's *enduo* meaning *sinking into a garment*. This verse speaks of the Holy Spirit coming at Pentecost with His empowerment.

- *Fire*—This is a consistent symbol of the Holy presence and character of God with the Holy Spirit bringing forth judgment to purge, purify, and make alive with passion (Acts 2:3; Isaiah 4:4). Fire brings light and warmth. It burns what is burnable and tests what is not. Fire cleanses what water and air cannot. The warmth of fire will keep you alive.

- *Wind or Breath*—Both wind and breath are unseen powers, but you can see the effects of each. The life-giving breath of God is regeneration power. The Holy Spirit is invisible as a person but the effects of His presence can be seen (John 3:8; Acts 2:1, 2).

- ***Guarantee***—A guarantee is a down payment; a pledge of more to come. It represents first fruits, a promise, and an assurance of the eventual complete payment (2 Corinthians 5:5). Ephesians 1:14 tells us that the presence of the Holy Spirit is the guarantee that assures the eternal security of the believer.

I find it comforting that one or all of these various symbols can be found in our everyday life. How simple the Holy Spirit has made it for us to recognize who He is and what He represents each and every day!

Notes

Chapter 10

The Duties of the Holy Spirit

"....He will take of Mine and declare it to you."
(John 16:15)

The Holy Spirit has various duties. It is important for us to understand what these duties are.

The Holy Spirit's duties pertaining to the universe.

The whole of the Trinity had part in creation. The example of this is when a person purposes to build a house. That person would hire an architect to draw the plans for the house, and a contractor to follow the architect's plans and build the house. This is the same with creation. The Father is the initiator of the universe, the Son is architect of the universe, and the Holy Spirit is the contractor who gets the work done.

We can see the Holy Spirit at work in creating the earth (Genesis 1:2), in creating the stars (Psalms 33:6), in creating the trees, birds, animals, and sea (Psalms 104:16-18, 25), and in creating man (Job 33:4).

The Holy Spirit's duties pertaining to the nation of Israel.

This is seen all through the Old Testament. The Holy Spirit came upon different individuals with His anointing to perform the tasks assigned to them. The judges, kings, priests, and prophets in Israel experienced the Spirit upon them and were known as the Lord's Anointed. The Holy Spirit came upon the tabernacle and temple of Israel. He led the nation of Israel through the desert. During the Tribulation He will come upon Israel, and during the Millennium the Holy Spirit will come upon them. The Holy Spirit has, is, and always will be active with His duties to the nation of Israel (Ezekiel 39:29). All those who experienced the operations and power of the Holy Spirit could give evidence that it was definitely *"...not by might nor by power, but by My Spirit, says the Lord of hosts."* (Zechariah 4:6).

The Holy Spirit's duties pertaining to the Old Testament.

The Holy Spirit was not available to all mankind in the Old Testament times. He was seen at work in creation and in the chosen nation Israel. The prophets did, however, clearly speak of the coming day when the Spirit would be poured out upon all flesh, both on the nation of Israel and the Gentile nations (non-Jews) at the same time (Joel 2:28).

The Holy Spirit's duties pertaining to the New Testament.

The prophecies from the prophets concerning the Spirit pouring out on *all flesh* was fulfilled at the death, the burial, the resurrection, the ascension, and the glorification of the Lord Jesus Christ. It would be His ministry to receive the fullness of the Spirit as the perfect Man, the Messiah of God, and then pour out the same Spirit upon all flesh and upon those who believe on Him unto eternal life. The gift of the Holy Spirit is available to all of us who accept the finished work of the cross, and then the Holy Spirit brings us from regeneration unto glorification (John 16:13, 14).

The Holy Spirit's duties pertaining to the life of the Lord Jesus.

The Holy Spirit's involvement is evident from Jesus' bodily conception to His final ascension. The whole life of Jesus as the perfect Man was governed by the Spirit.

- **Jesus** was born of the Spirit (Matthew 1:18-20; Luke 1:35).
- **Jesus** was anointed by the Spirit (Luke 4:18).

- **Jesus** was filled with the fullness of the Spirit (John 3:34).
- **Jesus** was sealed by the Spirit (John 6:27).
- **Jesus** was empowered by the Spirit (Luke 4:14).
- **Jesus** was led by the Spirit (Matthew 4:1; Luke 4:1).
- **Jesus** healed the sick by the Spirit (Luke 4:18).
- **Jesus** spoke and taught by the Spirit (Luke 4:18).
- **Jesus** cast out devils by the power of the Spirit (Matthew 12:28).
- **Jesus** sorrowed in the Spirit (John 11:33).
- **Jesus** rejoiced in the Spirit (Luke 10:21).
- **Jesus** was justified by the Spirit (1 Timothy 3:16).
- **Jesus** offered Himself at Calvary through the Spirit (Hebrews 9:14).
- **Jesus** was resurrected by the Spirit (Romans 8:11; 1 Peter 3:18).
- **Jesus** gave commandments to the disciples by the Spirit (Acts 1:2).
- **Jesus** baptized and empowered the Church by the Spirit (Acts 1:5, 8).
- **Jesus** directs and governs the Church by the Spirit (Revelation 2:7, 11).
- **Jesus** will return and raise the dead in Christ through the Holy Spirit (Romans 8:11).

After reading how the sinless Son of God found it essential to totally depend upon the Holy Spirit to structure every word and guide every step, how much more is this absolutely vital for the believer today? It is only as believers totally depend on the Holy Spirit that all God wants to do in and for him will be done.

The Holy Spirit's duties pertaining to the Scripture.
The Holy Spirit is the author of both the Old and New Testament (2 Timothy 3:16). He chose three basic methods in the preparation and production of His divine manuscript, the Bible:

- *Revelation*—This process flowed from God to man. The Holy Spirit spoke to 40 human writers of the Bible the message He wanted them to communicate.

- *Inspiration*—This process flows from man to paper. The Holy Spirit guided the writing of these 40 writers so that the spoken message would be accurately written.

- *Illumination*—This process flows from paper to heart. The Holy Spirit takes the written Word when it is read and taught and enlightens human minds who will hear it.

The Holy Spirit's duties pertaining to the non-believing world are very important to look at.

Just before Jesus entered Gethsemane He told His disciples He had to go away, but that because He was going, He would send the Holy Spirit to comfort them, and to convict the sinner (John 16:8-11). That word *convict* also means reproof in the Greek, to *convince of something*. The Holy Spirit will both convict and convince mankind...

- **Of sin**— because he rejected Christ's sacrifice on Calvary (John 3:16-18).

- **Of Christ's righteousness**—Paul wrote the whole book of Romans about this word righteousness. Paul points out, first of all, that God *is* righteousness. He points out secondly, that God *demands* righteousness. Lastly, Paul states that God *provides* righteousness.

- **Of future judgment**—The Holy Spirit points out to the sinner that all unsaved people belong to satan (John 8:44), that satan's doom is already in the making (Romans 16:20), and that all unsaved people will share satan's doom (Matthew 25:41).

Notes

Notes

Chapter 11

The Holy Spirit: Founder and Builder of the Church

"Now, therefore, you are no longer strangers and foreigners, but fellow citizens with the saints and members of the household of God, having been built on the foundation of the apostles and prophets, Jesus Christ Himself being the chief cornerstone, in whom the whole building, being fitted together, grows into a holy temple in the Lord, in whom you also are being built together for a dwelling place of God in the Spirit."
(Ephesians 2:19-22)

The Church was formed into a united body known as the Body of Christ by the Holy Spirit on the Day of Pentecost. Pentecost is called the birthday of the Church. On that day the Holy Spirit baptized into this spiritual body 120 believers who were waiting in unity for the Promise of the Father and Son after the ascension of Christ (Acts 2:1-4;

1 Corinthians 12:12, 13). From this point the Church went from 120 to 3,000 believers, and was added to daily (Acts 2:40-42). The Church is the people of God, not a building!

The Holy Spirit formed the Church to be the new and living temple of God, setting believers in their places as living stones in the New Covenant temple. The Spirit is the Executive of the Church and it is He who calls, quickens, energizes, and equips the believer for the various ministries in the Church (1 Corinthians 3:16; Ephesians 2:19-22).

The Holy Spirit brings direction, anointing, and illumination to the Church (2 Corinthians 1:21; Ephesians 1:17, 18; 1 John 2:27). It is the Holy Spirit who inspires worship and service in the Church (Philippians 3:3). The mighty presence and power of God are available for each service, but the pastor and congregation must welcome and allow the Holy Spirit full reign in the services.

The Holy Spirit wants the Church involved in mission work, and throughout the book of Acts He is seen directing that work. One example of this is in Acts 8:29: *"Then the Spirit said to Philip, 'Go near and overtake this chariot.'"* The Holy Spirit separated Barnabas and Saul for the ministry in Acts 13:2, 3. He directed the missionary journeys by telling them where they could and could not go (Acts 16:6-7, 10). The Holy Spirit desires to inspire the music to the Lord (Ephesians 5:18, 19). Many times where I am preaching, the praise and worship leader selects the exact songs that correspond with my message. This only happens when the preacher and the song leader allow the Holy Spirit to direct them as to what to preach and what to sing.

The Holy Spirit places and anoints the believers for the governmental offices such as apostles, prophets, evangelists, pastors, and teachers of the Church (Ephesians 4:11, 12). Jesus is the Great Shepherd of these governmental offices of the Church, and it is the Holy Spirit who appoints and anoints the under-shepherds of Christ. The under-shepherds oversee the people of God and are assigned by the Holy Spirit to feed them (Acts 20:28).

Many times man has appointed man, or man appoints himself to be an overseer or under-shepherd of the people of God, but this is out of order because Church offices are only appointed by the Holy Spirit; then they are accepted by man (Hebrews 5:4). I knew that the Holy Spirit, not man, had placed me as an evangelist to equip His people to do the work of the ministry. This knowledge keeps me strong and stable!

The Holy Spirit wants to make the decisions in the Church (Acts 15:28). The Council of Jerusalem that I mentioned earlier showed the teamwork between the local Church and the Holy Spirit as the Executer of the Church. The Church is not a democracy but a theocracy. The leadership and the members must hear what the Spirit is saying and deciding for the Church in order for it to be full of the power and presence of the Lord. The Holy Spirit will condemn or bless the Church's efforts as needed.

In Revelation 2:7 we are told, *"He who has an ear, let him hear what the Spirit says to the churches."* These words of the Spirit are written seven times in the beginning chapters of Revelation. When the Church starts putting top priority on **hearing** what the Holy Spirit is saying concerning how He wants to improve and correct the Church, it will not be so quick to allow the influence of culture or the world to penetrate it. The believers are the Church. The building is just that—a building—and it becomes the Church when the believer goes into it. I see so many churches run as an organization instead of an organism. This is very wrong!

The gifts and fruit of the Spirit are for the people of God. When a church allows the gifts of the Spirit to be manifested in the services, it is demonstrating the Spirit's omnipotence, omniscience, and omnipresence (1 Corinthians 12:4-11, 28-31; Romans 12:6-8). The fruit of the Spirit is the nature and character of the Spirit, and the members of the Church are to be manifesting the fruit of the Spirit (Galatians 5:22, 23).

Jesus is the head of the Church and He was totally submitted to and led by the Spirit, which allowed the Spirit to flow freely in perfect unhindered action. This same submission and leading of the Holy Spirit is of the utmost importance for the Church today if it is to function according to the Father's perfect will.

Notes

Notes

Chapter 12

The Holy Spirit's Activity in the Believer's Life
Part 1

"....He saved us, through the washing of regeneration and renewing of the Holy Spirit."
(Titus 3:5)

The Spirit brings about the born-again experience or new birth.

Jesus said to Nicodemus in John 3:5-6, *"...unless one is born of water and the Spirit, he cannot enter the kingdom of God. That which is born of the flesh is flesh; and that which is born of the Spirit is spirit."* Jesus was speaking of a spiritual rebirth. Peter says, *"...having been born again..."* (1 Peter 1:23). Paul declared this to Titus, in Titus 3:5: *"...the washing of regeneration and renewing of the Holy Spirit..."* Regeneration does not make a sinner a better man, but brings a new man. By faith the believer is made a partaker of the divine nature. I thank the Lord every day for this transformation in my life.

When a person is born naturally, natural life is imparted. In the beginning Adam and Eve were born of God, but both Adam and Eve lost spiritual life for themselves and for all mankind when they sinned. They lost the indwelling presence of the Holy Spirit. God had given them clear instruction about what they could and could not do in the garden, and warned that death would follow disobedience to His Word (Genesis 2:17). At the moment they ate from the tree of good and evil, they became self-conscious instead of spirit-conscious. As a result of their sin they were left in spiritual darkness as would be all of mankind after them.

Spiritual life is imparted to the believer through the indwelling Holy Spirit, which is the mark of a New Testament Christian (Romans 8:9). The simple definition of a Christian is to be "Christ-like." The human body of Christ was the dwelling place of the Holy Spirit, and the Holy Spirit indwells the body of a Christian in the same manner. Our body is the temple of the Holy Spirit, and it belongs to Him (1 Corinthians 6:19).

The Spirit brings assurance of the believer's salvation.

The word *salvation* in the Greek is *soterion* which is an all-inclusive word signifying forgiveness, healing, prosperity, deliverance, safety, rescue, liberation, and restoration. Christ's salvation is total in scope for the total man: spirit, soul, and body. This is the new birth and it is the Holy Spirit who assures the believer of sonship (Romans 8:16; 1 John 5:10; Galatians 4:6).

The Spirit indwells the believer's spirit.

This is in close relationship to the regeneration of a person by the Holy Spirit. The indwelling of the Holy Spirit is how it is known if that person belongs to Christ or not (Romans 8:9). The indwelling of the Holy Spirit also guarantees the believer's resurrection (Romans 8:11).

The Spirit speaks to the believer.

This is seen throughout Scripture. He speaks with direction to Philip in Acts 8:29. He speaks warnings concerning the latter times in 1 Timothy 4:1. He speaks guidance to the Church over and over in Revelation 2:7, 11, 17, and 19. These are just a few Scriptures where the Holy Spirit is speaking to the believer personally and to the Church corporately.

The Spirit opens the believer's understanding to the things of God (1 Corinthians 2:12).

The Spirit also teaches the believer, and guides him into all truth (John 16:13). Notice the word *all* is used; the Holy Spirit will not just guide into truth, but He will guide into *all* truth. Why? Because a half-truth is sometimes worse than ignorance. Full knowledge concerning God's Word is where the Holy Spirit guides the believer. Because the Bible is a spiritual book, the believer needs the Spirit to reveal hidden meaning, making its teachings clear, and causing freshness and meaning to come from even the most familiar passages.

The Holy Spirit reveals the things to come concerning spiritual blessings in the believer's life (1 Corinthians 2:10).

The Holy Spirit makes prophetic Scriptures clear, teaching the believer the dispensational truth concerning what lies ahead for the world and the Church (Amos 3:7; Genesis 18:17). The Holy Spirit guides and teaches the path that lies ahead of the believer, and whatever path is set before him, the Holy Spirit will help him be victorious. All teaching or revelation from the Holy Spirit will line up with the written Word of God, and He will teach and guide the believer into *all* truth (1 John 2:27).

The Spirit imparts life and brings strength to the believer's inner being (John 6:63; 2 Corinthians 3:6).

The word *life* in both of these verses in the Greek is *zoopoieo* meaning to *revitalize or quicken*. I am so glad we can have this revitalizing in our life continually by the person of the Holy Spirit. We are "*...to be strengthened with might through His Spirit...*" according to Ephesians 3:16. The word *strengthened* in the Greek is *krataioo* meaning to *empower* or *increase in vigor*, and the word *might* in the Greek is *dunamis* meaning *miraculous power* and *ability*. Into the believer's inner being, the Holy Spirit will bring that increase in vigor and give him miraculous power and ability to live here on earth victoriously doing the will of the Lord.

Notes

Chapter 13

The Holy Spirit's Activity
Part 2

"...that He would grant you, according to the riches of His glory, to be strengthened with might through His Spirit in the inner man..."
(Ephesians 3:16)

The Spirit enables the believer to pray.

Prayer is a vital part of the believer's life. It is sometimes hard to know what to pray, but the Holy Spirit knows! Only when we allow the Holy Spirit to direct our prayers will those prayers be effective (Romans 8:26-28). Another way the Holy Spirit enables the prayer is found in Jude 20. When a believer prays in the Holy Spirit, he gives his inner self a boost over the flesh, allowing faith to arise.

The Spirit enables the believer to worship in spirit and truth (John 4:23, 24).

The word *worship* in this verse is *proskuneo* in the Greek and means to *reverence* and *adore,* and this can only be done by the Holy Spirit giving the believer's spirit the ability to worship. Worship must be in the Spirit and not in the flesh (Philippians 3:3).

The Spirit leads the believer (Romans 8:14).

The Apostle Paul uses the word *sons* in this verse. The word *sons* speaks of mature children of God who have learned that if they are to be led by the Holy Spirit, they must be obedient and follow Him. When first saved we are infants but through reading the word and growing in the Lord we become mature. The believer is commanded to walk in the Spirit and be guided by the Spirit (Galatians 5:25).

The Spirit enables the believer to put fleshly deeds to death.

We will only be able to have victory over the flesh by having our mind set on spiritual things and by the power of the indwelling Holy Spirit (Romans 8:5-6). The Apostle Paul uses the word carnal in this passage meaning *fleshly* which tells us it is impossible to do the will of God and put fleshly deeds to death with a carnal mind (Romans 8:13). The Holy Spirit enables the believer to put the deeds of the flesh to death by reckoning the old man crucified with Christ

(Romans 6:11; Galatians 2:20). The Holy Spirit wants the believer to live a victorious life, but in order to do this the believer must choose to live under the guidance and direction of the Holy Spirit. Every day we have a choice—to follow the Holy Spirit or to follow our flesh. The way we choose determines if we will be a victor or victim.

The Spirit produces Christ-like character and fruit in the believer's life.

The Holy Spirit transforms the believer into the image of Christ (2 Corinthians 3:18). Like a mirror that reflects, the child of God is to reflect the glory of God. Moses asked God to show him His glory (Exodus 33:18) and God responded by telling him that He would make all His goodness pass by him (verse 19). The word *glory* in Hebrew *is kabod* meaning *weight,* or *splendor.* In the Greek it is *doxa* meaning *dignity* and *honor.* The word *transformed* in the Greek is *metamorphoo* meaning *changed.* The English word is *metamorphose* and the definition found in Webster's is *to make over* to a *radically different form, composition or disposition.* By the operation of the Holy Spirit the child of God is being made over to have a radically different form in composition and disposition so he will show the world Christ's character and reflect His glory which is goodness, honesty, dignity, and honor.

The Christ-like character is also seen when the Holy Spirit produces His fruit in the believer's life. This is the ultimate goal of the Holy Spirit here on earth (Galatians 5:22, 23). The fruit of the Spirit is placed within a person by the indwelling presence of the Holy Spirit at the time of regeneration. Fruit does not just appear fully grown on a tree; it takes time for fruit to mature, and this is the same with the child of God. By coming under the guidance and power of the Holy Spirit, the believer will produce the pleasant full-grown fruit of the Holy Spirit reflecting Christ-like character.

The Spirit calls the believer for special service.

The Holy Spirit sets the believer apart and sends him out on special assignments. The brethren then come in agreement with the Holy Spirit by laying hands on and praying for the one being set apart and sent out (Acts 13:2-4). The Holy Spirit gives the believer the special ability he needs to victoriously complete whatever special services for which He has set him apart and sent him to do. Spiritual ministry and service is always accomplished by the Spirit of God, not human ability (Zechariah 4:6).

The Spirit empowers the believer to witness.

I've heard people say, "Witnessing is not my thing. I just do not know how." Every believer received the Holy Spirit at his new birth and if he submits to the

Spirit, the believer will bear fruit. However, to be an effective witness for Christ, the Spirit must come *upon* him bringing His gifts and power (Acts 1:8). The word *witness* in the Greek is *martus* meaning *martyr*. A martyr is one who is willing to die or make a great sacrifice for a cause. The believer's cause is Jesus Christ. The Early Church disciples suffered great persecution as do many disciples today. Jesus knew that His people would need power in order to witness for Him. The power needed to witness or be a martyr for the cause of Jesus Christ only comes when the Holy Spirit comes upon the believer.

The Spirit imparts spiritual gifts to believers as He wills.
The whole Trinity is involved in giving gifts, but after Pentecost the Holy Spirit began His gift-giving to the believer (1 Corinthians 12:4, 7). At salvation the Holy Spirit comes to dwell *in* the believer, and at Pentecost the Holy Spirit came *upon* the believer, and He came bringing His gifts as answer to the promise of Christ. It is very important not to mix up the Person of the Holy Spirit with the gifts He brings.

The Spirit will bring about the resurrection and immortality to the believer's body in the last day (Romans 8:11).
The Holy Spirit will change us, getting us ready to be resurrected (1 Corinthians 15:51, 52).

The Holy Spirit has duties to perform in a believer's life. God has given man free will to choose, so it is the believer's choice to submit fully to the Holy Spirit and allow Him to bring him from the starting point of the new birth to a mature powerful man or woman of God, moving in the Spirit realm instead of the flesh realm.

> *"If the Holy Ghost is indwelling a man or woman, no matter how sweet, how beautiful, how Christ-like they are, the lasting thought you go away with is —what a wonderful being the Lord Jesus Christ is."* --Oswald Chambers

Notes

Notes

Chapter 14

Enemies of the Holy Spirit

"Anyone who speaks a word against the Son of Man, it will be forgiven him; but whoever speaks against the Holy Spirit, it will not be forgiven him, either in this age, or in the age to come."
(Matthew 12:32)

The Holy Spirit is working in the Church and in individuals to bring forth the character of Jesus Christ. This requires full cooperation with His activities. When Christians are not following God's ways, then an enemy or sin abound. Webster's dictionary defines *enemy* as one that *attacks*, is *hostile*, or *tries to harm another*. Here are key enemies opposing the work of the Holy Spirit:

- *Satan*—He is the number one enemy of the Holy Spirit. Satan is a created being and is not omnipotent, omniscient, or omnipresent. He can create nothing.

He can only take the things of God and counterfeit them (1 John 4:3). Where there is truth, one will always find a counterfeit.

- **Demons**—These are false prophets with false spirits; wicked spirits and unclean spirits that want to lead the believer down the path of destruction. Demons are assigned to the believer to deceive, while the Holy Spirit is given to the believer to lead (Matthew 12:43-45; 1 John 4:1, 2). The book of James says a man is led astray by his own desires and then enticed. The word enticed is to bait, as if baiting a hook to go fishing. Demons have hooks baited with temptations which are enemies to the Holy Spirit's plan and purpose.

- **People of the world refusing sanctification**—Jesus went to the cross and shed His blood so the Holy Spirit could come and sanctify all the people of the world, but the people of the world continue to refuse to have the Holy Spirit set them apart and make them righteous (1 Peter 1:2; 2 Thessalonians 2:13). A person's refusing quenches the Holy Spirit's ability to bring sanctification, serving as an enemy to the Holy Spirit (1 Thessalonians 5:19).

- **The flesh**—The flesh lusts against the Spirit (Galatians 5:17). Webster defines *lust* as a longing or desire for something that promises enjoyment or satisfaction. Lust can also be defined as an active desire resulting from the diseased condition of the soul (*one's mind, will, and emotions*). This was brought about by the fall of man in the Garden of Eden and sin entering the human heart.

The Holy Spirit demands that the believer control the lust of the flesh (Ephesians 2:3).

It is our responsibility to remember we are children of God, not children of wrath, and to submit all fleshly desires to the Holy Spirit. The Spirit dwells in the believer so he can overcome the flesh (Romans 8:9).

The fruit of the Spirit is an antidote to the works or lust of the flesh (Galatians 5:19-22).

In this Scripture, the works of the flesh are listed right before the fruit of the Spirit to make it easy to recognize which we are walking in. At conversion the Holy Spirit indwells us, making it possible to produce His fruit. Fruit is grown and it takes time to mature. It is only as we allow the Holy Spirit to increase our knowledge of God that we can be fruitful in every good work (Colossians 1:10).

The Spirit has made us a new creation in Christ with a new relationship with Christ (2 Corinthians 5:16, 17).

I am so grateful to the Holy Spirit for making me a new creation and giving me a new life.

Notes

Chapter 15

Baptism with the Holy Spirit

"John answered, saying to all, 'I indeed baptize you with water; but One mightier than I is coming, whose sandal strap I am not worthy to loose. He will baptize you with the Holy Spirit and fire."
(Luke 3:16)

Through the years there has been much controversy concerning the baptism of the Holy Spirit. We must understand what the Holy Spirit meant when He penned through men the words of John the Baptist in Matthew 3:11 and Luke 3:16: *"... He will baptize you with the Holy Spirit and fire."* The word *baptize* in the Greek means *to make fully wet* or *to immerse,* and the word fire represents the physical manifestation of God's presence seen throughout the Bible. So being baptized with the Holy Spirit and fire means that the believer is immersed into the physical manifestation of the magnificent oneness with the Holy Spirit.

The baptism with the Holy Spirit is a powerful experience which was responsible for the miraculous growth of the Christian Church in the apostolic and post-apostolic years, and has been the primary cause of the dynamic revival that has swept parts of the world since the turn of the 20th century. This empowering of the Holy Spirit changed my life and gave me the power to overcome addictions and many other issues.

The empowering ministry of the Holy Spirit is not above the redemptive work of Christ. The principle work of the Holy Spirit is to exalt Christ. But Christ's finished work makes provision for fullness of the Spirit beyond regeneration.

When regeneration occurs in a person, the Holy Spirit dwells *in* him, but after regeneration a believer can choose to be baptized with the Holy Spirit and the Spirit comes *upon* him. *"But you shall receive power when the Holy Spirit has come upon you…"* (Acts 1:8).

Jesus Christ is the baptizer with the Holy Spirit, and that baptism is the vital connection to the spiritual life and service of every believer.

What the experience of baptism with the Holy Spirit is NOT:

- **It is not the SECOND BLESSING.** This term is not used in Scripture. The believer is to receive all the blessings of God at salvation.

- **It is not the SECOND DEFINITE WORK OF GRACE.** This term is not in the Bible, but the believer should continue to grow in the grace of God.

- **It is not HOLINESS.** Holiness describes a quality of character and it has to be developed.

- **It is not SANCTIFICATION.** The Holy Spirit does sanctify the believer, but the baptism with the Holy Spirit is very different.

- **It is not a REWARD** for Christian service or to make a Christian spiritually superior to others, but believers were to expect this experience to come upon them right after conversion. It is also available at any stage in our walk with the Lord!

What the Baptism with the Holy Spirit IS:

- **It is something to USE and not just to HAVE.**

- **It is an experience that was poured out once on the Day of Pentecost and is available to ALL Christians today.** This experience is available for each believer after conversion, but we must want to receive this baptism and ask Jesus for it (Acts 2:1-4).

- **It comes after salvation and it is a definite spiritual experience.** In the New Testament this experience is seen as a sudden supernatural anointing with power and energy with the Holy Spirit *coming upon, falling upon*, or *poured out upon* a desiring submitted believer, equipping him for special service.

- **It is the promise of the Father** (Luke 24:49; Acts 1:4). The promise of the Father concerning the Holy Spirit coming with His baptism is for every seeking, submitted believer.

- **It is a gift** (Acts 2:38). The word *gift* in the Greek is *dorea* meaning *gratuity*. A gift is given and not earned or purchased so the Holy Spirit is a gift given to the believer who in turn must simply want and desire to receive. The gift of the Holy Spirit must not be confused with the gifts (Greek *charismata*) that He brings with Him to give to the believer.

- **It is an experience which Jesus commands every believer to receive** (Acts 1:4-11; Mark 16:17). This is a direct command of Jesus Christ Himself to the believer, so for a believer **not** to be baptized with the Holy Spirit is to walk in disobedience to Christ.

The baptism with the Holy Spirit is necessary and purposeful. It gives POWER for Christian service.

This is the first and most important purpose of this experience for the believer. Jesus gave this key instruction to the believer just before His ascension (Acts 1:8). The word *power* in this passage in the Greek is *dunamis* meaning *a force, miraculous ability, or miracle worker.* Jesus was born of the Spirit but He was also anointed with the Spirit before He began His public ministry (Luke 4:18). Jesus did mighty works while He was on the earth but He tells believers that they would do greater works than He did (John 14:12). This scripture is talking about the quantity, and not the quality, of the works the believer will do. On the Day of Pentecost the disciples were transformed into different men and women when the Spirit came *upon* them, and so will believers today be given that transforming miraculous ability when the Holy Spirit comes *upon* them. We all need the *dunamis* of the Holy Spirit!

It gives POWER for spiritual warfare.

We are sent out to do a spiritual task that will require us to have spiritual power to accomplish it. Human ability will not help us when we are wrestling with the devil and his demons (Ephesians 6:12). Spiritual warfare is not about people here on earth, but it is about what is going on in the *heavenly places*.

Spiritual warfare is vital not only for the believer but for those around him. Jesus said the believer would have a river of God's blessing flowing out of him to others (John 7:38, 39). The Father and Jesus Christ have provided the spiritual ability needed for us to defeat the enemy in the heavenly places and have the rivers of blessing flowing from us to others by the *dunamis* of the Holy Spirit!

It gives POWER ability.

At the point of conversion, a power starts to work within us giving us abilities (Ephesians 3:20). The person of the Holy Spirit is the power working *within* us. When we go a step further to the baptism with the Holy Spirit who comes *upon* us, we receive the *dunamis* power or miraculous ability coming from spiritual gifts given to us by the Holy Spirit. This miraculous ability will help us when we are being persecuted for the Lord's sake. It will give every believer the ability to live a holy life in a corrupt world. This power ability helps him do the work of the Lord willingly, lovingly, faithfully, and with fervency until Jesus comes.

Notes

Notes

Chapter 16

Gifts of the Holy Spirit

"Now concerning spiritual gifts, brethren, I do not want
you to be ignorant."
(1 Corinthians 12:1)

The Church (Body of Christ) has been in a state of progression since its birth at Pentecost. The beginning of the Church was considered apostolic Christianity because of its simplicity, fellowship, evangelism, and love. It had no formal organization and it had no membership roll or building to maintain. It was simple and the teaching was easy to understand. Christians took care of the needs of others in the Body. The faith of these new Christians made them want to help the oppressed and poor, just as Jesus taught.

The key to the growth of the Church was the believers' firm understanding of the resurrection of Jesus Christ. The

Apostles, along with others, had proof of the bodily resurrection of Christ and His ascension. They witnessed the Lord being on earth for 40 days after the resurrection and before His ascension. This knowledge passed on to next generations through verbal testimonies and writings. The Church went through great persecution and even went into a time called the Dark Ages where it became corrupt and very far from the original teachings of Jesus Christ, but also far from the Person of the Holy Spirit and His gifts.

The Holy Spirit gives revelation (2 Peter 1:12).

He desires all God's people to be established in *truth*. Men and women have given their lives for what the Church is today. Revelation is given to appropriate truth. Revelation happens when the Holy Spirit illuminates and brings applicable reality to a scriptural truth in a sovereign way. It is our responsibility as believers to lay hold of it by faith and fulfill it. God does His part, and the believer must do his part.

We want to bring to light that not only mature Christians can move in the gifts, but also babes in Christ. Jesus released His own disciples before they were fully matured. Paul sent letters to the Corinthian Church addressing issues concerning incest, lawsuits, fornication, marriage and divorce, eating food offered to idols, and the Lord's Supper. They were carnal, and babies in Christ, yet Paul knew that the gifts of the Holy Spirit are an intricate part of every believer's equipment, and believers would not lack or come short in any of the gifts of the Spirit (1 Corinthians 1:7). Paul even tells them not to be ignorant of the gifts (1 Corinthians 12:1). We are the generation that has been given the revelation of truth concerning the Spirit's gifts; we are the generation responsible to establish every saint in the gifts the Spirit gives.

Three chapters of the New Testament, as well as parts of two others, are devoted exclusively to the subject of the gifts of the Spirit. There are approximately one hundred New Testament references on the subject of spiritual gifts, or on the exercise of one or another of those listed in 1 Corinthians 12. There is not the slightest inference in the New Testament that any gifts of the Holy Spirit would cease before seeing our Lord *face to face* and before *that which is perfect is come* (1 Corinthians 13:10, 12).

Believers are to expect the special enablement of spiritual gifts in order to carry out the divine mission committed to them by the Lord Jesus Christ. Jesus instructed believers then and now to be endued with power from on high (Luke 24:47-49). On the Day of Pentecost visible and audible signs were present, and all those gathered began to speak in other tongues (Acts 2:2-4). Wherever the early believer went he was marked by the supernatural and the Spirit's power.

The believer today is as much an ambassador for Christ as the early believer, and the same equipping of supernatural divine power is available to us today.

In 1 Corinthians 14:12, we are told that the purpose of the spiritual gifts is for the edification, or building up, of the Church to profit all. *"Let all things be done for edification."* (1 Corinthians 14:26). The word *edification* in the Greek is *oikodome,* meaning *building up.* The word *profit* in the Greek is *sumphero* meaning *contribute or advantage.* Spiritual gifts are to be used for the spiritual advantage and building up of the whole Body of Christ (1 Corinthians 12:7).

The spiritual gifts are also to give testimony of the risen Christ (Acts 4:12-26); provide spiritual ability greater than natural ability (1 Corinthians 2:4); inspire a reminder of God's presence and power (Matthew 28:20); cause the Body of Christ to function (1 Corinthians 12:12-14, 27); and are a convincing sign to unbelievers (1 Corinthians 14:4, 22).

The Holy Spirit's gifts are characterized by infinite variety. They are not computer program cards inserted in believer robots always producing identical results. Just as there is a variety of gifts, there is a variety in the manifestation of each gift because of the believer's God-created individual uniqueness (1

Corinthians 12:4-7). The word *manifestation* in the Greek is *panerosis* meaning *exhibition* or *expression.* This lifts the gifts or *charisma* of the Spirit out of the realm of the natural. The gifts exhibit a showing off of the divine revelation concerning the supernatural given freely to the believer. The categories and meanings of specific spiritual gifts of the Holy Spirit are given to us according to His will (1 Corinthians 12:8-11).

Notes

Chapter 17

Gift of Utterance – Tongues

"...to another different kinds of tongues, to another the interpretation of tongues."
(1 Corinthians 12:10)

The word *tongues* in the Greek is *glossa* meaning *language,* specifically *one not naturally acquired.* The gift of tongues is a supernatural verbalization by the Holy Spirit in a language that is not learned by the speaker nor understood by the speaker. It is a language spoken somewhere here on earth or in heaven. This was first manifested in Jerusalem, and it is available to all believers who want to receive the gift of tongues.

When a believer is baptized with the Holy Spirit, he will speak with the gift of tongues as a sign showing he is fully immersed with the Holy Spirit.

There are two different manifestations of the gift of tongues.

1) **The private devotional tongue is a tool to be used by the believer.**

> This refers to tongues given at baptism with the Holy Spirit. This gift is for every believer and every believer is commanded to have this gift. This is the tongues that Jesus spoke of when He instructed the disciples concerning the Great Commission; He gave these instructions after His resurrection and right before His ascension back to the Father from where He came (Mark 16:17, 18; Acts 1:8). These were some of the last words Jesus spoke to His disciples. Jesus commanded the disciples then and every believer since to avail themselves of the supernatural capabilities needed to fulfill the mission set before them.

> This devotional, or private, language is a tool for the believer to live a victorious life while on earth; we will not need it in heaven. The Bible has many scriptural reasons why the believer is commanded to have this gift active in his life, and they are the following:

- **Jesus commands it in the Great Commission.** After His Resurrection and before His Ascension (Mark 16:17).

- **Tongues is the initial sign of the Baptism with the Holy Spirit.** This was given at Pentecost (Acts 2:4).

- **Tongues is for personal, spiritual edification.** This will give a jump start and a building up in the believer's spirit (1 Corinthians 14:4).

- **Tongues remind the believer of the Spirit's indwelling presence** (1 Corinthians 14:4).

- **Praying in tongues helps the believer's weakness or his inability to be productive** (Romans 8:26).

- **Praying in tongues, the believer will always be praying the perfect prayer** (Romans 8:27).

- **Praying in tongues will keep the believer's prayer in line with God's will** (Romans 8:27).

- **Praying in tongues stimulates faith.** It builds the believer up in faith over the flesh (Jude 20).

- **Praying in tongues, the believer is speaking not to men but to God.** He is speaking the mysteries of God (1 Corinthians 14:2). The mysteries are the things hidden from before the foundations of the world which are now seen in the Person of Jesus Christ. Now it is *Christ in you the Hope of Glory* speaking the mysteries of deliverance, healing, salvation, peace, joy, etc. No human language could ever express all that Jesus Christ is in the believer!

- **Praying in tongues will tame the tongue.** James 3:8 says man cannot tame the tongue, but when the believer uses the natural tongue to speak with the supernatural gift of *tongues,* the natural tongue **will** be tamed. He will speak blessings and the promises of God instead of evil and corrupt things.

2) **There is a different tongue used in public ministry.** This gift is **not** given to every believer but as the Holy Spirit wills. The private devotional gift of tongues is given to the believer before the public gift of tongues is given.

- **This tongue is a sign to the unbeliever (1 Corinthians 14:22).** This happens in two ways. First, the powerful deliverance of a message in tongues accompanied by the interpretation of it may surprise and speak to the unbeliever. Second, when tongues are spoken, the unbeliever might know the language and understand clearly what the Holy Spirit is saying.

- **This tongue is for the spiritual edification of the Church.** When a message in tongues is given, someone must be present who will give the interpretation of the message which then equals the gift of prophecy (1 Corinthians 14:5; 1 Corinthians 14:26-28).

Notes

Chapter 18

Gift of Utterance – Interpretation of Tongues

"...to another the interpretation of tongues."
(1 Corinthians 12:10)

The word *interpret* in the Greek is *diermeheuo* meaning *expound* or *explain thoroughly*. The gift of interpretation of tongues is the divine, supernatural ability to interpret a message given in tongues. This interpretation is not a direct translation of the utterance in tongues but a Spirit-revealed interpretation of a message from God. The interpretation may vary in length from the utterance in tongues. It is just as supernatural as tongues in that the interpreter has no understanding of the message; he speaks the interpretation directed from the mind of God. Those who have the gift of tongues are admonished to pray for the gift of interpretation. *"Therefore let him who speaks in a tongue pray that he may interpret."* (1 Corinthians 14:13).

This gift is the least of all the other gifts because it depends on another gift to be in operation. Its purpose is to bring understanding of the gift of tongues to the hearer (1 Corinthians 14:5). The gift of interpretation is also to be used in the private devotional tongue used in prayer (1 Corinthians 14:13-15).

The use of this gift should be done in an orderly manner (1 Corinthians 14:26). The interpretation of a message in tongues will always lead the hearer toward the things of God and not away!

Notes

Notes

Chapter 19

Gift of Utterance – Prophecy

"...to another prophecy..."
(1 Corinthians 12:10)

The gift of prophecy is a divinely inspired utterance in a known language. It is the speaking forth of the mind of God in a general assembly and its purpose is for edification (building up), exhortation (stirring up), and comfort (1 Corinthians 14:3). Paul tells believers they must extend their faith to prophesy, and He also says that all can prophesy one by one (Romans 12:6; 1 Corinthians 14:31).

Statements concerning prophecy include the following:

1) Tongues and interpretation together equal prophecy.
2) The Hebrew word for *prophesy* means to *flow forth*. This carries the thought... *to bubble forth like a fountain*.

3) The Greek word for *prophesy* means to *speak for another*. It means to speak for God or to be His spokesperson with His divine inspiration.

4) Prophecy may be defined as the simplest form of inspired utterance.

5) The gift of prophecy is <u>not</u> a repetition of Scripture verses.

6) The gift of prophecy is <u>not</u> preaching. It requires NO PREPARATION, where preaching does.

7) It is a GIFT of prophecy, <u>not</u> an OFFICE of the prophet.

8) There is also a SPIRIT OF PROPHECY (Revelation 19:10). This is a gift also and not an office, but an anointing arising from Christ within the believer that takes place on occasions of special anointing. This manifestation comes on those who are not prophets or do not have the gift of prophecy and who normally do not prophesy; but when the spirit of prophecy is present, they may do so. It is a time of special provision by the Spirit and frequently happens under one of three conditions:

- When a mighty prophetic presence of the Lord permeates the service, making it easier to prophesy than to keep silent.
- When people come to a company of prophets or under the mantel of an anointed prophet.
- When people are challenged by the minister to let God arise and testify through them by the spirit of prophecy.

We must know the safeguards against prophetic deception. Just as the Spirit "bears witness" or testifies with the believer's spirit that he is a child of God (Romans 8:15), in the same way the Spirit can help the believer know if what is being done or said is of God or not.

The prophecy itself and the spirit in which it is given is to be tested by qualified leadership (2 Corinthians 13:1). The Bible clearly shows that prophecy should be judged by leadership. This does not hinder the flow of the Spirit but it will fine tune the believer and keep him accountable.

The believer has the written Word of God. If the prophecy is tested against Scripture and is found to be free of scriptural and doctrinal error, it is received as inspired by God. Every believer should be encouraged to become more and more grounded in the Word of God which will give less opportunity for error. A balance is needed between sufficient faith in the Holy Spirit to allow Him free operation and sufficient obedience to the Scriptures to "prove" the gift. The Spirit-Word balance is attained by the grace of God alone.

Notes

Chapter 20

Gift of Revelation – Word of Knowledge

"...to another the word of knowledge through the same Spirit..."
(1 Corinthians 12:8)

The word of knowledge is the supernatural revelation by the Holy Spirit of certain FACTS in the mind of God. These facts can be about the past, present, or future. It is an instant knowledge about a fact from the Lord that the recipient has no way of knowing except from the mind of God. It is a word from God's infinite knowledge about the earth, humanity, or the universe. It is a word of God's knowledge for a need at a particular place, for a particular purpose, for a particular season or time, or for a particular person or people. It is a fact that can warn of danger to come, or to expose hypocrisy or deception!

Jesus used this gift when telling the Samaritan woman at the well that she had five husbands (John 4:17, 18). As a direct result of the use of this gift by Jesus, the woman ran and called others telling them about the man who knew everything. This was not so, Jesus did not tell her all, or know all; He gave her a word or a fact concerning her life.

Some of the uses of the word of knowledge:
- A fact concerning the thoughts of men's hearts,
- A fact concerning men's plans or motives,
- A fact concerning the past, present, or future,
- A fact to warn of coming danger, *or*
- A fact to expose hypocrisy or deception.

The word of knowledge is manifested many different ways. This gift can come to the believer in a vision or a dream, by a definite impression, from the inner voice of the Spirit, by an audible voice, from an angel, or it may come by the quickening of the Scriptures. The gift of the word of knowledge and the gift of the word of wisdom working together produce good fruit.

Notes

Notes

Chapter 21

The Gift of Revelation – The Word of Wisdom

"...for to one is given the word of wisdom through the Spirit...."
(1 Corinthians 12:8)

The word of wisdom is not wisdom in general. It is a word or a fragment of God's wisdom. The word of wisdom is the supernatural ability of the Spirit to impart special and specific insight, guidance, or counsel, which brings life-changing illumination.

The word of wisdom will bring a response such as, *What made you think of that? That is the very thing I needed to hear; or, Thanks for that word; it helps me solve my problem.* It normally deals with the future and reveals a glance into the hidden realms of God's future plans and purposes. It is not for the unfolding of God's revealed will in His Word, but for the unfolding of His unrevealed word, and the declaration of His hidden purposes apart from His Word, but CONFIRMED by His Word.

This is a special gift given as a word of wisdom differing from natural wisdom or divine wisdom that is available for everyone (James 1:5). This gift can come to the believer in the same method that the word of knowledge comes. Jesus operated in this gift when speaking to the rich young ruler, and the discussion between them ended suddenly when the young man was faced with an almost unexpected, immediate, life-changing decision (Luke 18:18, 22).

Notes

Notes

Chapter 22

The Gift of Revelation – Discerning of Spirits

"...to another discerning of spirits..."
(1 Corinthians 12:10)

The word *discern* in the Greek is *diakrisis* meaning *to separate thoroughly*. The gift of discerning of spirits is the supernatural ability to see into the three realms of the spirit—the kingdom of darkness, the kingdom of light, and the human spirit. It is the Holy Spirit communicating the motive or origin of an action, attitude, or an atmosphere. It is being able to detect the Lord's divine leading and presence, demonic activity in people or in geographical locations, or human motives that would cause a person to act or think a certain way.

The discerning of spirits in its limited function has been understood as the ability to identify specific evil spirits and their devices. It is a safeguard against deception. In

1 Thessalonians 5:21, we are told to *"Test all things; hold fast what is good."* This gift is **not** fault finding or reading minds; it has nothing to do with psychic phenomena, and it is not related to psychiatry.

Some of the ways this gift is manifested are:

- Evil spirits or angels seen in a vision.
- To see and discern the name, the operation, and even the location of a spirit.
- Have a quickening within one's spirit.
- Feel the presence of the demonic activity, such as a heaviness in the chest area or the hairs standing up on the back or neck.
- Feel the presence of angelic activity, and it can manifest with a calm joy or overwhelming awe.
- Different odors can be manifested, both demonic and angelic.
- Physical symptoms can be manifested such as headaches or nausea, so strong that a person will have to leave the area.

We live in a very demon-infested world just as Jesus did. He used this gift of the Holy Spirit and we need to also. It is our job not to allow the demons to cause us or others to be their victims. Using this gift will help us be victorious in this world.

Notes

Notes

Chapter 23

Gift of Power – Faith, Healing, and Miracles

"...to another faith by the same Spirit, to another gifts of healings by the same Spirit, to another the working of miracles..."
(1 Corinthians 12:9-10)

The gift of faith is a supernatural surge of faith in the heart of the believer to confidently believe God and/or speak for God.

> It is a special *faith*. This faith is not saving faith or the normal Christian faith given to the believer at conversion. Special faith works often in conjunction with healings and miracles. This gift is more passive than active. It operates by *receiving from* the Spirit, while the working of miracles *does things by* the Spirit.

An example of this can be seen when Moses parted the Red Sea for the Hebrew people to cross. He had to receive from the Spirit a special surge of faith that went beyond his normal faith for the working of miracles to operate through him. In many Scriptures the reader can observe the gift of faith in operation before the gifts of healings and the working of miracles will be manifested.

The gifts of healings is a supernatural manifestation by the Holy Spirit to heal injuries, handicaps, and diseases without the aid of natural medical care or human means.

It is not to be confused with scientific, medical, or surgical skills. Healing gifts may operate by word or by touch or in rare cases such as Peter passing by and his shadow healing some (Acts 5:15).

In the Greek both the terms *gifts* and *healings* are plural. This fact suggests that there are many gifts of healing for different diseases, and that each exercise of the healing power is a separate gift. This can be received by a believer's own faith (Mark 11:24). This is between the believer and God. Healings are manifested through one believer to the other, or from a believer to a non-believer. The healings can be instant or come in the process of time.

Gift of the working of miracles is the supernatural intervention in the ordinary course of nature.

It is an interruption of the system of nature as we know it. It is a supernatural manifestation by the Spirit, which is sovereign by nature and not bound by any natural law. The working of miracles means acts of power such as raising the dead, producing water from a rock, and turning water into wine.

Jesus started His public ministry with a miracle by turning water into wine (John 2:7-9). This gift was operating when Jesus invited Peter to walk on the water with Him (Matthew14:29). The greatest observation of this gift is when a person receives salvation.

During my journey with the Lord I have seen and been part of watching the Holy Spirit bring about all His gifts. I have experienced crooked arthritic hands straighten instantly by the supernatural intervention of God. I've seen blind eyes be able to see, and ears that couldn't hear, be able to hear instantly. I've seen cancer instantly gone. Believers and nonbelievers alike need the people of God to use the Holy Spirit's gifts. Lives will be changed, including your own, if you get on the path of the Holy Spirit, which is action!

Instructions given by the Apostle Paul concerning spiritual gifts:

In 1 Corinthians 12:1 Paul writes, *"Now concerning spiritual gifts, brethren, I do not want you to be ignorant."* The word *ignorant* deals with the mind and the Greek word is *agnoeo,* meaning to *lack intelligence, information,* or *comprehension.* The antidote for ignorance of spiritual truths is a mind renewed with the Word of God. *"And do not be conformed to this world, but be transformed by the renewing of your mind..."* (Romans 12:2).

Paul goes on to say in 1 Corinthians 14:1, *"Pursue love, and desire spiritual gifts, but especially that you may prophesy."* The word *pursue* in the Greek is *dioko,* meaning *press toward* or *follow.* The word *desire* in the Greek is *zeloo,* meaning *to covet* or *to be zealous for.* Paul tells the believer that the zealousness for spiritual gifts must follow the path of love.

A believer is to desire to prophesy, because this gift will bless a lot of people at the same time, but Paul is not saying it is more important than the other gifts. Paul also says if a believer does not want to comprehend and intelligently understand the spiritual gifts, to allow them to stay ignorant! *"But if anyone is ignorant, let him be ignorant."* (1 Corinthians 14:38).

143

Notes

Chapter 24

Conclusion

"However, when He, the Spirit of truth, has come, He will guide you into all truth...."
(John 16:13)

The Person of the Holy Spirit is the third person of the Godhead. He is co-equal and co-existent with the Father and the Son. We are living in the dispensation of the Holy Spirit, but He can be seen throughout the Scriptures from Genesis through Revelation. He is for all mankind, but brings conviction to the unbeliever concerning his unbelief in Jesus Christ. He is the instrument in regeneration and sanctification. As a believer we must get acquainted with the Holy Spirit, know Him personally, and allow ourselves to be good soil for the planting of eternal truths concerning Him.

The Holy Spirit proceeds from the Father and always glorifies Christ. One of His chief missions is to reveal the virtues, power, and love of Christ. We can rely on the Holy Spirit to guide us in truth because He is the Spirit of truth. The Holy Spirit is changing us into the image of Christ daily. He has a marvelous personality and brings divine illumination with revelation to us concerning the Scriptures. He is the witness in our spirit that we are a child of God. He is the one that will help us be victorious in life. He is the one that will show us how to do spiritual warfare, not only for ourselves but also for others.

The Holy Spirit feels, thinks, teaches, and comforts. He is Omnipotent, Omniscient, Omnipresent, and Eternal. He is the author of the Holy Bible which was penned by men whom He inspired. Down through the generations the Holy Spirit has dealt with the children of God, trying to lead and guide them. In the Old Testament, God's people did not have the Person of the Holy Spirit living inside them to guide them, but in the New Testament it is clearly seen that He dwells within the believer.

The disciples in the Early Church knew how to obey the unction of the Spirit living within them. The Holy Spirit directed their path so they could complete their part of the Great Commission given by Jesus. *Go into all the world....* It is now the responsibility of the believer today to live in truth and fulfill the Great Commission. *Go into all the world....* The Holy Spirit has given us His fruit for growth in character, and His gifts as the power tools needed to complete the task set before us victoriously. The Holy Spirit has done His part; now we as believers must do our part.

Once again the question; *Is the Holy Spirit alive in the world today?* After your study of this book, I believe you will have no doubt that He truly is alive and active, influencing the events of our world and especially our very lives.

After learning about Him, it becomes every believer's responsibility to follow the path of the Spirit and activate His power for the people and situations we face daily. What an awesome privilege and responsibility.

Notes

About the

Author

In addition to writing books, Judy pens a monthly column for a secular newspaper and an occasional article for Christian publications. She is an ordained minister, and preaches throughout the United States, additionally serving as a Chaplain for Campers for Christ. Judy's education in the Word of God is extensive, and she has earned a Doctorate Degree in Ministry of Theology.

If you have questions, are in need of guidance, or would like more information about Judy's books or *Good News Ministries*, you may reach her at the following addresses.

Dr. Judy Baus can be contacted *through* **GOOD NEWS MINISTRIES, Inc.**:

Dr. Judy Baus
Good News Ministries, Inc.
9309 99W Highway
Gerber, CA 96035

baus1@juno.com   www.judybaus.org

Notes

Notes

Notes

Made in the USA
San Bernardino, CA
20 April 2017